A Special Night

A Coloring Book

by
Joe Pileggi

Illustrated by
Sabrina Ferriera

WHP
Wyatt House Publishing

Mobile, Alabama
www.wyattpublishing.com

Wyatt House books may be ordered through booksellers or by contacting:

Wyatt House Publishing
399 Lakeview Dr. W.
Mobile, Alabama   36695

Because of the dynamic nature of the Internet, any web address or links contained in this book may have changed since publication and may no longer be valid.

Cover and interior layout by: Mark Wyatt

ISBN 13: 978-1-954798-10-6

Dedication

This book is dedicated to six future world-changers—my grandchildren:
Raygan, Stella, Liam, Asher, Nathan and Jonah.

Look out world, here they come!!

"Look at the stars, Grandpa Ram. I tried to count them but there are too many. I ran out of numbers."

Grandpa Ram just smiled at me and then looked up at the sky with me.

"Yes, there are a lot of stars up there," he said.

There was no moon so it was a very dark night, except for the stars.

"Have you ever tried to count them?" I asked.

"Yes, I have Aren. When I was about your age," he answered with a light pat on my head.

"How many are there?" I was so excited to hear his answer that it was hard for me to stand still.

"I don't know. I tried to count them several times. But, I ran out of numbers too."

Wow, I thought. There must be a lot of stars up there if Grandpa Ram ran out of numbers. He knew a lot more numbers than I did.

"How did they get there?" I asked.

"Someone made them – a long, long time ago."

"Really? WHO?" I said, getting more excited by the minute.

"Well, He's been called by a lot of names, but most call Him God!"

"God? He made all the stars? Where does He live?"

The questions kept coming faster and faster.

"A place called heaven," Grandpa Ram said as he pointed toward the sky.

"Way up there, past the very last star."

I gazed at the stars in the sky and wondered to myself, "Gee, I wonder which one is the last one? They all look so far away."

I looked at Grandpa Ram and asked, "Have you ever seen God?" Of course not, I thought. Why did you even ask the question? If He lives behind the last star, how could anyone ever see Him?

"Yes, I met Him once. It was quite an experience," Grandpa Ram laughed as he looked at me. I must have looked funny as I stared at him with eyes as big as saucers.

"It's true," he said in between chuckles. "Do you want to hear the story?"

I was so stunned I couldn't talk, so I just nodded my head as I thought, "Now this I gotta hear!"

"Well," Grandpa Ram began, "It was a night much like tonight: lots of stars, very dark. I was just a lamb then, about your age."

I was so excited I jumped to my feet. I could hardly stand it. I asked questions one right after another without taking a breath.

"You saw God when you were my age? What did He look like? Was He tall? Did He have a …"

"Well, let's not get ahead of ourselves," He said in a calm voice. I think if Grandpa Ram didn't interrupt me I might have exploded with excitement.

Grandpa Ram continued, "I'll tell you that part in a minute, but something else happened first."

Grandpa Ram had a big smile on his face as he remembered that night.

"What happened?" I asked, trying to keep myself calm.

"Do you see that field of grass over there?" He pointed toward a hill where we were often led to eat grass.

"Yes, I see it. Why?"

"Well, that's where we were when it happened. It was a cold night, so all of us lambs were laying close to each other so we could try to be warm. All of a sudden, the sky got light as day."

I was confused. "But Grandpa Ram, you said it was night. How could it be as bright as day?"

"Well, Aren, do you remember the storm we had the other night, with all the lightning?"

"Yes, I do. It was scary"

"Well, that's how light it got that night, only it didn't flash and go away like lightning does. It stayed light for a long time."

My eyes got big again. "It did? Were you scared?"

"I started to be, but there was something different about this night. It was exciting, yet peaceful. That's because the light was coming from a whole bunch of angels."

My mouth dropped open to match my eyes. "Angels?" I asked.

"Yes. They really scared the shepherds who were taking care of us." He giggled as he said it.

"But, then the angels told them not to be afraid because they had good news to tell them. They said a baby had been born that night in the town of Bethlehem."

"That's where we're from!" I said excitedly. "It's right there." I pointed to some buildings with dim lights coming from them.

"Yes." Grandpa Ram continued. "Not only that. They told the shepherds the baby was born in our stable, where we live when the shepherds bring us back from the field."

"Our stable?! A baby was born in our stable?" That was my home. I was born in that stable.

"Yes. In a manger."

"The manger? You mean that long thing the shepherds pour grain into for us to eat?"

"Yes, that's it." Grandpa Ram answered.

"Ew…YUK! That's not very clean," I said as I wrinkled my nose up and shook my head.

"I know, but that was the only place they had. There wasn't any room in the hotel. So the angels told the shepherds where the baby was."

"Did the baby have a name?" I asked.

"Yes. The angels said He was Christ the Lord." Grandpa Ram's voice was shaky, like he was going to cry.

"What's the matter, Grandpa Ram?"

"Nothing, Aren, my son. Nothing. That night, that baby, was so special. It brings tears to my eyes every time I remember it."

Christ, the Lord. There was something about that Name. It was like I had met Him too. But that wasn't possible. Grandpa Ram was only a lamb then and I wasn't even born yet.

"But you said you saw Him, Grandpa Ram. You couldn't see Him from the field over there if He was in the stable manger over there," I said and I pointed in opposite directions.

"That's right. But after the angels left and it was dark again, the shepherds said to each other, 'Let's go see this thing the angels told us about!!'"

"So they left us in the field and they all walked toward Bethlehem – and the stables. I don't think I was supposed to go with them, but I really wanted to see this baby. I followed them, hoping they wouldn't see me."

"Come. Let me show you where I saw the Baby."

We began to walk slowly, almost too slowly – so I decided to run ahead because I couldn't wait to see where the Baby was. I didn't get far, because I got out of breath. Grandpa Ram chuckled as he watched me stop and try to catch my breath.

Soon, Grandpa Ram caught up with me. He was still laughing.

As we continued, Grandpa Ram continued his story: "It seemed like a long walk, even for my little legs. But I was too excited to be tired. The shepherds walked faster and faster the closer we got to the stables. It was hard for me to keep up."

"But, you know what, Aren? I began to feel warm, even though the air was cold."

"Was it because you were trying to keep up with the shepherds?" I asked.

"I thought so at first," Grandpa Ram answered. "But it wasn't."

"Then, what was it?" I didn't like mysteries. I wanted to have answers to my questions.

"The Baby," he said softly.

I stopped walking and stared at him. "But how could…" I couldn't even finish the question.

"I don't know, Aren, but it was true. Here we are at the stables."

We stood on the path that led into – and out of – the stable. This is where we came to eat, be cared for by the shepherds, and to stay when the weather was rainy. It was a big building made out of wood, with a roof, but no walls. Inside the stable were rows of mangers, the big "dishes" we ate out of. They looked like cradles, but they weren't for babies. We each had our own manger that was filled with grain or hay for us to eat. I had my own manger.

"This is where the baby was born?"

"Yes," said Grandpa Ram. "In one of these mangers."

"Which one?" I asked, trying to guess which one before he told me.

"Come, I'll show you."

We walked down one of the rows of mangers. I could see mine – at the end of the row. Grandpa Ram continued to walk down the row, but he wasn't talking now, almost like he didn't want to disturb the quiet. I wondered when he was going to stop and show me the manger where the Baby was born. But he didn't, until he came to the very end of the row, where my manger was. He turned to me and said quietly, "This, Aren. This is where the Baby was born."

"But Grandpa Ram, this is MY manger. This is where I come to eat every day," I cried.

"Yes, I know. And it is no accident that it is. I wanted this to be your manger, so I made sure the shepherd gave this one to you." Grandpa Ram smiled, but I saw he had tears in his eyes.

"I stood right where you are standing now when I first saw Him. There was a glow, a light around Him. And that was why I felt warm in the cold air. It wasn't like a fire warm, it was more like a warm on my insides, a peaceful warm. As I looked at Him, I was sure He smiled at me." Tears were running down Grandpa Ram's face, but he was still smiling.

"But, why did you want me to have this manger…His manger?"

"Because I wanted this night to come, the night when I would tell you the story – His story. To know His story is to know Him. And to know Him gives you life, life that will never end."

I didn't really know what he meant by that, at least not yet. But now, knowing that the Baby was born in my manger, I really wanted to meet Him. But how? And when?

"I sure would like to meet this Baby sometime," I wished out loud to Grandpa Ram. "He must be so cute."

"Oh, He's not a Baby anymore, Aren. He's all grown up."

"He is?" I asked, my eyes wide with wonder.

"Yes, and you have already met Him." Grandpa Ram said.

"I have? When?"

"Maybe this will help you remember," Grandpa Ram said with a sneaky smile. "He is called by many names today. But we sheep know and love Him as Good Shepherd."

I couldn't speak for a while. Tears came to my eyes. "Good Shepherd?" I finally asked, my voice shaking. "The One who saved me from the lion after I ran away from Him? He was the Baby that was born in MY manger?"

Grandpa Ram smiled and nodded as the tears ran down my face. I cried for a long time as I remembered how bad I had been running away from Him and how He came and saved me anyway, holding me in His arms, fixing my broken leg. I could still see His smile and hear His soft voice telling me how much He loved me.

"I really would like to see Him again," I said between sobs. "I want to tell Him how much I love Him."

"I think He knows," Grandpa Ram said. "As far as seeing Him again, He is going to be in a near-by town in a few days. I can take you there if you'd like."

"Oh, yes, Grandpa Ram. Would you? I shouted, jumping up and down.

"Yes, son, I will. Now let's get some sleep. It's really late."

"OK, Grandpa Ram," I said. "And, Grandpa Ram, thank you for telling me the story of Baby, …er… Good Shepherd."

"You're welcome, son. I know your dreams will be sweet tonight," said Grandpa Ram with a smile. I knew they would be, too. But, first I had to do something I had never done before. I climbed into the manger and laid in the hay to sleep – just like Good Shepherd did when He was the Baby. My thoughts and dreams came together as I fell asleep. I was sleeping in the manger that Good Shepherd had slept in as a Baby. I felt closer to Good Shepherd than ever before, even though He wasn't there. I could feel His love all around me, and I thought, "It's true. There really is No Greater Love!"

Mr. Joe was raised on a dairy farm in New York State. He grew up loving animals, and still does. He lives with his wife, Lori, and has 3 grown children and 6 grandchildren.

Sabrina Ferriera was born and raised in California. Sabrina is an artist whose inspiration and passion is focused on neature, especially animals. Her dream has been to use her talent to glorify God and to spread the Gospel. She currently lives in the San Francisco Bay area.

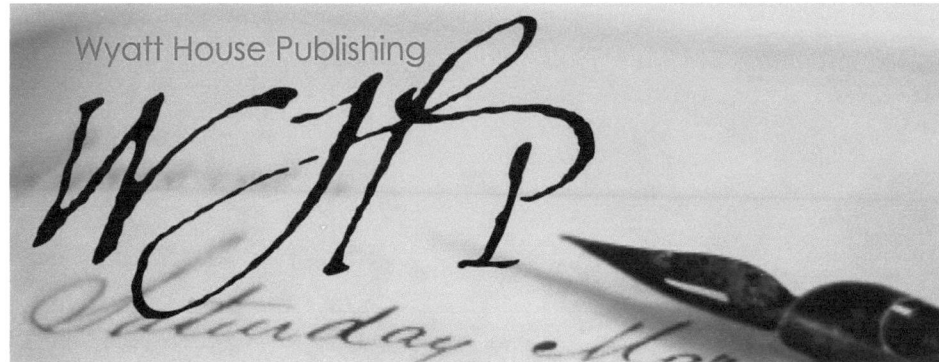

Wyatt House Publishing

You have a story.
We want to publish it.

Everyone has as a story to tell. It might be about something you know how to do, or what has happened in your life, or it may be a thrilling, or romantic, or intriguing, or heartwarming, or suspenseful story, starring a cast of characters that have been swimming around in your imagination.

And at Wyatt House Publishing, we can get your story onto the pages of a book just like the one you are holding in your hand. With professional interior design and a custom, professionally designed cover built just for you from the start, you can finally see your dream of being an author become reality. Then, you will see your book listed with retailers all over the world as people are able to buy your book from wherever they are and have it delivered to their home or their e-reader.

So what are you waiting for? This is your time.

visit us at

www.wyattpublishing.com

for details on how to get started becoming a
published author right away.

www.ingramcontent.com/pod-product-compliance
Lightning Source LLC
Chambersburg PA
CBHW041155040426

42445CB00007B/151

9 781954 798106